PRESENCE OF MIND

First published in 2005 by
The Dedalus Press
13 Moyclare Road
Baldoyle
Dublin 13
Ireland

www.dedaluspress.com

© Dolores Stewart & The Dedalus Press, 2005

All rights reserved. No part of this publication may be reproduced in any form or by any means without the prior permission of the publisher.

ISBN 1 904556 40 X (paper)
ISBN 1 904556 41 8 (bound)

Dedalus Press titles are represented and distributed in the USA and Canada by Dufour Editions Ltd., PO Box 7, Chester Springs, Pennsylvania 19425, and in the UK by Central Books, 99 Wallis Road, London E9 5LN.

Front cover image by Michael Boran
Design by Pat Boran

Printed in Ireland by ColourBooks.

The Dedalus Press receives financial assistance from An Chomhairle Ealaíon / The Arts Council, Ireland.

Presence of Mind

Dolores Stewart

ACKNOWLEDGEMENTS

Grateful acknowledgement is made to the editors of the following in which a number of these poems originally appeared: *Poetry Ireland Review, The Honest Ulsterman, Criterion, The SHOp* and *Anon.*

Contents

Ein Winterabend	1
Portrait of an Artist	2
Triptych: Circus Beckman	3
Plato's Cave	6
The Jazz Singer	7
Off the Record	8
Spencer's Folly	10
Aftermath	11
Wild Geese	12
Christchurch, Middle England	13
Digbeth Bus Station 10 pm	14
St. John's, Nottingham	15
Holyhead Blues	17
Wittgenstein in Connemara	18
American Wake	19
Epiphany	20
Detour	21
Child on a Swing, 1922	22
Maryville, Winter, 2001	23
Meeting Place	24
Ashram	25
Antigone's last stand	26
Corona Borealis	29
Homo Ludens	30
Danse Macabre	31
Triptych: Belshazzer's Feast	32
Nemesis	35
Soul Talk	36
Waking the Dead	37
Reading between the Lines	49
Tableau	50
The Home Stretch	51
La Lutte avec l'Ange	52

Death of Socrates	53
Double Take	54
Heidegger's Silence	55
Wrong Address	56

Higher than the lark,
Ah, the mountain pass!
—quietly resting.

Matsuo Basho, *1644-1694*

Ein Winterabend
after Trakl

Speaking out, the poet tries flesh and bone on the snow
Ghosting the window at the close of day, soundlessly
Mouthing as vespers in the distant village
                    fall on ears more attuned to
The crunch of muffled footsteps coming up the pathway
Towards the waiting house. Inside, the table is set
For those who have not yet arrived, whose feet will stamp
Quickened enigmas between the wrought-iron garden gate
                    and the chequered tiles
In the hallway. What is not yet said is the greeting, the grace
Before meals, the compline of bread and wine resting still
On the linen tablecloth. What is never said
Is the final word, the habit of a lifetime given over to silence.

Portrait of an Artist

Blindfolded, you hold your hands out
Like sensors in the dark that might
Have been day, that might have been a dream.

Elsewhere you're the one in evening dress
Training binoculars at the night sky,

The novice blowing bubbles at the moon,
The jazz musician (so it seems)
With saxophone or drum.

Always, you're the trapeze artist teetering
On the brink, a close call in the space
Between the double somersault

And the upturned faces. Again, you blow the horn
As of old expecting a trace that rebounds
To the sound of your self. Settle for black lines.

Triptych : Circus Beckmann
after Max Beckman, 1884-1950

1. Self-Portrait in Tuxedo, 1927

So, you're nobody's fool. More a *grand seigneur*
On one of your frequent outings to a five star hotel.
Caught at an angle, you look down on the world
You've conjured up, going to ground
In the breeze playing on monochrome drapes
Behind you, as if there was nothing to be seen,
As if this were the cue for your second début.
But if it wasn't for light filtering through
The open window, you would have been invisible
In the brushstrokes that show you in tuxedo
And evening suit, with something of a ringmaster
In you, and something of a clown. A balancing act
Between the fingered cigarette and the ash, a face
Made up out of shadows. Half-cast.

2. Greasepaint & Sawdust

It was the clowns most of all they came to see
When the circus came to town, knowing for sure
That the gonzos would have them rolling
In the aisles, breaking their sides laughing; worth
Every stitch to see them pulling faces at the ring
Master and bantering a way out of bottlenecks
& logjams to change the carnival water into wine.
Grinning from ear to ear, they bend bottoms up
To pop hoses from balloons, laughing long and loud
At the shrieks and squirms, the tickled minds
Of the pundits who knew nothing else so much
But that this was an act, an exercise in fun and games
That couldn't go wrong. Not in this parade ring.
And not unless the clowns turned. Upside down.

3. Circus Animals

With every crack of the whip, the bagged line
Up and lumber around the ring, or mount
Three-legged stools for the eyes of those in the know,
And paying. Fancy looking for a way out
Through a wall of rigged applause and box-office
Takings that count on them for kicks, turning over
The same tricks for punters eating their hearts out.
Holding the whip hand, you pimp the fix
From a distance and watch the lights go down, barring
The lit cigarette and eyes in the dark. Nothing
On your mind beyond a quick turnabout of the night's
Caravan and the signs of a full house. Beyond
A nod and wink at the ghouls pulled by the star line-up
Making ready for the road. Drummed on.

Plato's Cave

Call them pot-heads, dogfaces, grunts. Nicknames.
No way will they make it out alive, become
Who they are in the midday sun.

Mesmerized by the magic, you dwell in shadows
Cast by the fire that somebody out there is stoking
In the kingdom of spin.
                      Never mind that rats
Marauding in the pits show up only as animal extras
In the frame. Or that there are days when
The screenplay strikes you
                      as too contrived, and you listen
To canned laughter, pulling on a fag for comfort,
And wait for the next showing. Like cats' eyes,
You don't miss a trick
                      in the splattered graffiti
Of darkness where, behind the scenes on any given day,
The crew works itself into a lather pitching grey on grey.
But all you know of light
                      fits onto the wall of a cave
That enthralls you; where a look over your shoulder
Is out of the question in a script missing an exit line.

The storyboard unfolds to the scriptwriter's whim.
You act the part. Sing dumb.

The Jazz Singer

Not before time, he moves to the rhythm
Of the limelight, moving from music into
Naked song.
                    How every note
Settles into place like gold-dust
Gracing arrangements on the monochrome
Page.
                      How audience
And performers lock together in concert,
In raw praise.

Off the Record

From the word go, there was always somebody game
To nail space onto paper, the contours
Of landscape, a line measuring distance between two

Points, height above sea level. A star to go by. Pale
In tone but revealing in a certain light a mapmaker bent
To the task, drawing tilted lines to the letter of the law,

The stamp of settlement leaving nothing to chance
In the register of place. As it stands.

By any yardstick, the perfectly preserved fingernails
Of the long-buried body somehow brought to light
In a summer bogcutting should not have been there

In the first place. Or upended by the random harvest
Of a mechanical digger throwing off the habit
Of a perfect crime: lost bearings, a severed breath,

Burial of sorts in a bottomless boghole, a *caveat* of absence
Beyond the boundary line. By the way.

As the crow flies. Six inches to the mile and *every danceing
Meadow, ditch and quirribog* showing up
Higgledy-piggledy as playthings to the naked eye

Are sworn statements laid down on sheets, part and parcel
Of barony and townland where hardly an anthill escapes
The gridmarks, not even the light of day shackled by timid

Windowpanes or smoke signals pitching for the lie of the land,
The shirt on a body's back. For what it's worth.

❧

On the face of it. But watch, off limits, where the talk breaks
Through and goes for a song. There, or thereabouts.

Spencer's Folly

I see him, hellbent on horseback, his poet's eyes
Digging into the flank of a language

That left its mark on the thin gruel
Of the winds that schooled him –

A master saddler on the bareback land, his
For the *cock-of-the-walk* taking.

And I see him riding free-rein and roughshod
Over the bones of an old poetry

Beggaring the scorched earth of his verses
And, thrown

I see him run for cover and cower
In a fox's den, with nothing left

Except a bolt towards the blocked door
That only a lackey knows.

What words can spur you now, or slip
The blinkers of your knackered eyes—

Your hobbled bones a metaphor
For the death rattle you listened for,

Your gaping mouth tethered
To the silent turfing of worms,

Your scudding words unleashed,
Coming back to haunt you.

Aftermath

Walter of the beads and rosaries, Aodh mac Aingil
Of the scholar's slate, Tadhg Gaelach of the ha'penny songs –
All famished. Euery one gone.

Who will buy a poeme *cia do cheinneóchadh dán* Now that
The wynde has died doune and the calendar daies outnumbered
To enclowd the dark secrets of the errant-runners, the braggarts?
Who will buy a poeme Now that the great oakwoods haue been felled,

The game and cuckoo-song banished from ancient Aherlow; Now
That the poets are forced to beggar them selues as rymers pencilling
Soured sonnets to the livery of Popingyes wont to playe the king,
Bending the knee to new Customes of mimicry and rime; Now

For the moste parte at a loss to offer Sanctuarie to the wylde wordes
Al of a scatter lyke dandelion floss counted out in hovrs of the clock
And outlawed lyke a swarme of Gnats from the Bog of Allen:
The canker of contrarie Speache granted thus to halter and sword,

To the machinations of those with a trick or two up the sleeve,
The knave, the black heart, the ace of spades. On my worde.

NOTE
Ceist! Cia do cheinneóchadh dán / Who will buy a poem – written by
Gaelic poet Mathghamhain O hIfearnáin, early C17th.

Wild Geese

On the plain of Aughrim, a lone wolfhound stands
guard over its slain master
                              in a field
of corpses fallen prey to voracious wolves covering
themselves in blood and changing forever the tenor
                                of their throats:
draining the life from the veins of a starry night.

    ❦

Mind you, whether you remember all this, all
you've been told
                              from the beginning
is neither here nor there. What matters is
that something of the texture remains
                              as a stepping stone
on which you traverse the frenetic streams
that crisscross your path, and the odd threads
of memory
                              that rip you up
from time to time, seeming to startle you, right
or wrong, with all the longing of a Jacobite song.

Christchurch, Middle England

No matter which way the wind blows,
No matter which way I turn, no matter
Which hour of the day—

I come face to face with a hunch
Hooked onto hightailed weathervanes
Atop cruciform village churches, still
In working order, still lording it
Over the seasons, the airbrushed questions.

This was no local Guernica, no Leningrad
Or El-Alamein. No winners or losers
Stonewall the flesh and blood figures moving
Through the matchstick landscape,
Ghosting some unnamed loss.

The butcher, the baker, the candlestick-maker...

No matter which map I read,
There's the *so-what* of triumphant drums,
The pyrrhic redbrick streets.

Digbeth Bus Station, 10 p.m.

Through half-closed eyes, I finger a winter's day
On granite slopes, the fall of light hallowed
By mist, rockpools sprayed by farflung particles
Of God and a sunset coming through in crimson
To raise traces of filigree in the grey –

A far cry from this, the half lit darkness
Of an underground bus station,
This cavern of disembodied voices
And cold rising from the guttering,
This sharp intake of breath,
This time of night.
      What price
The swept waiting rooms,
The waiting to be picked up passengers
Prowling around on the outside,
Coaches pulling in and out in a hurry,
The long-drawn-out sigh of concrete settling
Down on the shoulders of Methusalem?

For all I know,
Every damned road in the world feeds onto the M1
And every carrier of the word scribbles
Back to front markings on fogged up windows:
Final destination unknown.

St. John's, Nottingham

It wasn't as if the sun's threaded path
had led us to the door

or that the subliminal chatter of the Lace Market
had, in a moment, reverted

to old accents haggling over appliqué sprays
of rose and leaf,

or that the stalls chalked out for the horsetrading
at Bridlesmith Gate had shifted.

But this door opens onto no chancel or nave
and the patrons are no gargoyles grinning

over shoulders nor Cromwell's soldiers
bickering over stabling for their horses,

and not even the perfectly preserved stained glass
can cast doubt on this state-of-the-art bar,

a showcase of good taste in the face
of declining numbers and disbelief in ritual.

Still.

Something was left hanging, some
vagabond god allowed to tiptoe around

on the landlord's say-so, begging
for a share of the action.

*As to when it was that the sureness of touch
on old piano keys faltered and fell silent*

*and the sound of drumming
was heard distinctly in the distance*

is anyone's guess.

Holyhead Blues

Where, if you're Irish, it's always three
in the morning and the town, within earshot
of the mail train from London Euston,
is always sleeping;

where night workers rub
bleary signals out of the small hours;

and queues, like forgotten boithríns,
dock in silence past the gloved eyes
of the port police, and whatever

passes for a nod;

where night cranks on board, and turns in—
with lazybeds in mind—

to stake out the chances of a sunrise
in the West, in a pitch for lost time.

In your dreams.

NOTE *Bóithrín: a country lane*

Wittgenstein in Connemara

knew about the things that couldn't be said
even before he came, before sitting it out by the quiet
of a turf fire or fiddling with wordknobs
on the wireless. So it rains or it doesn't rain.

Time and weather notwithstanding, he
will make his way, dumbstruck, along rainwashed
slopes on some unerring path towards a faint
illegible hand that takes his breath away.

*Keeping his distance, the coastguard sees it all
through the hand-wiped glass of the window pane—
you feeding the birds like a latter-day St. Francis, winds
letting rip at ninety miles an hour, seagulls stalling*

*in mid-air, a lichened windowsill scattered with crumbs
for the famished, the circle of wild cats closing in
for the kill while your back was turned fathoming
language in oceandeep silence.*

Some kind of messenger, they said, fit for nothing
(they said) but gazing at the etchings of a broken stick
on a mountain track and reading the sheet music
playing to the gallery in his head.

In no time at all, crocus and snowdrop will come
to test his eyes at the sight of colour slipping
from the backbone of a mackerel sky in spite of this:
his insistence on second thoughts, on winter.

American Wake
for Peter Ward, Coolough, Galway & Boston, Mass.

He's walking the land again, maybe for the last time, marking off
The mearing walls by heart, the language no different from the Gaelic
Spoken in a Boston pub when the chairs were pitched out of the way
To nail the map back home to the floor, for fear of missing a trick
In the swivel of the index finger.
                                        Or the fist.
What he's driving before him are the livestock of his memory,
Their swishing tails playing him to a padlocked barn and unscoured
Milk churns waiting to be filled.
                                    By and by.
Why he goes to the trouble of fixing a new lock onto the farmyard gate,
Or hiding the antique plough beneath a tangle of blackthorn
After he'd taken it out to size it up as he'd done when it was new
To the earth and shy of furrows is a riddle to mind old bones, the likes
Of tenant and landlord both—

Sir Valentine the Sunday man
On the run from summonses and writs
Six days a week,

Or the last of the Clanricardes
Eating his dinner out of creased newspaper
In Regent's Park,

Lost for want of the rent.

Like seldom told ghost stories herded into meadows of night, and
Sidestepped now, he shrouds the holding and goes, making himself
Scarce, flying out from Shannon, maybe for the last time. For keeps.

Epiphany

For a split second, I saw the genealogy
Of my dead mother in his blue eyes, that day
His last in Sylaun Bog beyond the Curragh Line,
That day when some small significance took him

By surprise and shifted his attention to a detail
He hadn't reckoned on, and you could see
The dammed up words throbbing in his eyes, and
Catching him unawares, spilled out

As *smithereens* onto the bog floor after
He'd turned his back and, gutted, began again
To gauge the angle that had somehow escaped him
In the fraction between *dúchán* and cutting.

My mother too in her day would have believed
In those old stories about bottomless bogholes,
Of space beyond the measured foot, a missed step

And shrillness echoing like bevelled stones
Skimmed across rippled water
And then sinking into the silence, beyond reach.

NOTE *Dúchán: a small stack of turf*

Detour

Give me the word and I'll indicate just beyond
Kilcummin Churchyard for the turn-off to Machaire Mór
And pick up the road there
                          with telltale signs
Of a railway track and what remains of the gatekeeper's lodge.
What you'll see more than likely is a woman in black
With dimpled earrings looking past you,
                             her eyes humming
To the sound of someone she's been waiting for. All day.
Longing for a glimpse, she leans forward before settling,
Shoulders back, into the freckled tones
                             of an Edwardian photograph.
If it's later when we arrive, you'll hear my father
In fine voice giving a rendition of *Love's Old Sweet Song*
Or something from *The White Horse Inn*,
                             see his head
Raised in silhouette, their stillness in his face rising
To the high notes, the held breath working out variations
Within the score along the taut coordinates of song.
                             What do you say?
We can, of course, choose not to go there, bypass
The turn-off, bless the sleepers from us, drive straight on.
Just give me the nod. Say the word.

Child on a Swing, Oldchapel, 1922

Whenever I see you now, I see a child
Swinging in a country garden, waiting

For familiar handwriting and the hoped-for
Invitation to leave home,

The railway cottage laced by dawdling
Mailtrains and windfalls.

Years later, you remembered that day—
All fingers & thumbs—tearing open

The letter when it came, your sister's
Fallen face. Now

When I visit you in the old people's home
Your face lights up in instant recognition

Yet your memory cannot place me, and
You swing from sentence to unfinished

Sentence, casting around in silence
To find the words to say over and over:

"But you're ours, you're one of ours".

Maryville, Winter, 2001

Through those Alzheimer's eyes
your old worn walking stick becomes an object
of wonder, a page written in an old script
or a bead on your rosary—
signposts to a meaning staring you in the face.

Photographs surround you, immune images
from the world you've let go of, your memory
a rusty valve that unexpectedly opens—

and you remember, you remember an uncle
on your mother's side, the American judge
who came down hard on a word, insisting

on emphasis on the train to Galway
in the days before Wall St. wiped him out.
And you remember, you remember as if

it were yesterday, the day the Black & Tans
came to Oughterard and you hid
with your sister behind a breathless hedge.

*I admit the space between us, the train
waiting at Platform Five,*

*the muffled sounds of those out and about
and heading home,*

the world beyond you…

as, finally, you decipher that old script and grip
the walking stick, humming an old music hall tune
while keeping time on the way to an immaterial world.

And you smile, you smile.

Meeting Place

My heart sinks
As you fumble for a *one time* syntax
In the trickery of your old age—

                    You, the scavenger
Of words seeking to piece together
The riddle that bedevils you,

I, the onlooker
Sifting for clues in the clouds. Both
Of us at a loss. Wordless.

Ashram

Listen. Would anyone happen to know
Why such a guru would undertake such a journey
And end up with nothing to say? And
Would anyone care
              to tell why so many
Came running out of breath to hang onto his every word,
Having heard the rumours (yes, it was said)
That he knew everything about all there is to know,

The narratives of black holes, dark matter and all
The foibles of the vaudeville? Or, would anyway dare
To say what he proclaims in the dried-up riverbed
Of talk?
           By any reckoning, some measure
Of eternity had seeded by the time he stood up to leave,
Leaving them lost to the run of themselves, looking
To find the tongue in the subtext of silence. So to speak.

antigone's last stand

*Antigone she tutted, yes she tut-tut-tutted
As the king he strutted all over the town,*

*And the body it rotted, yes it rot-rot-rotted
As the sun came up and the sun went down.*

On the town. Downtown.

❧

A chorus to curse him, the pygmy king.
Siberian windgall to his upstart face, a pickaxe
Cast to his eye. Be warned.

Before this night is out, I'll show this so-called
King a thing or two, I'll rob his phony edict
Of its power

And bury, by the high light of the North Star,
My brother killed in noble fight

And left to rot on a dunghill. See if I don't
Burn the word of a king to ashes.

❧

A palette of banners for the new king.
The dazzle-scarves of the morning star
Anoint his brow and hopskip

Out over the ribbonbows, draft-
Horses of applause cantering
Across meadowfields of sweeteners

Fed from the royal hand, paper-chains
Sending ripples through the massed ranks
Of the hard of hearing, the also-ran.

❧

Now Antigone took a stand and proceeded
As planned to envelop her brother

In a winding sheet of sand, while the king
Took a look, took a long hard look, as the sun

Went down on the town. Downtown.

❧

Antigone like a chickenbone
In the royal throat, giving the lie to his words.

A fly in his mouth. Antigone in his face
Courting the death rap

For shredding the king's writ; a skylark
Stalled in the hawk's sight, nothing between them

But clapped air, the clamour of cupped wings,
A trained eye. Going in for the kill.

Her words swinging like windbreaks,
Her hanging body a grey crow:

A lantern hinging on the doorjamb
Showing up the ragged clothes

Of the king, drawing him outwards
From threadbare shadows, coming out

Into his own: *the talk of the bloody town.*

Corona Borealis

With eyes wide open, Ariadne turns
In on herself, turning her back
To the open door and the sound of
Receding footsteps.
                                   She's aware of sunfall
Surfing the mosaic floor, a hairline
Crack in the pillar.
She's aware of blackening sails, a pull
On the ocean, the onset of evening.
                                   Soon, she will turn
To stone, as statues do in the dead of night,
Sinking deep into her own ground.

Sorrowful…
               est anima mea.

How many hours have passed
Since she first took, between forefinger
And thumb, a single strand of thread
And laid it carefully
                                   on the labyrinth floor
Weaving for his feet a bridge to bear
The weight of his *hope-against-hope?*
When Theseus absconded,
He brought with him
                                   her store of words,
The spun thread. With verbs dying
On her lips, she had no way of telling how
                                   her name would constellate
In the heavens, a *benedictus* bearing into space
The *mot juste*. A say in the matter.

Homo Ludens

Everything rests on the clown
With the big mouth bursting to tell.
             Through raised stakes,
His memory quivering on the pirouette
That cost the Baptist his head, all
Circus paint and slapdash, he spins
                 like a wild cat
Into the market place, making a play
For the latest word: a scripted silence casting
Doubt on his trick-o'-the-loop pitch
                     which takes no notice
When his mouth, bubbling with vowels, spits
Acid brackets around the *crying-out-loud*
Of the crowd:

"If God is indeed dead, who then
Can we blame for the endless weeks
Of rain, the exorbitant price of bread?"

Danse Macabre

Swept off his feet by the music of all souls,
The teasing he swears by, Nietzsche
(Unhinged) dances like Dionysius in a space

That panders to the temper of his padlocked
Room. Whether or not the earth turns
On its axis is another day's work, a world

Turning on the word. Quickstepping,
He stops only to catch his breath and check
The glass for a second glance at the likeness

Jack-knifing in its frame, the bloodsucker
Who peers back at him dying for something
To say in tongue-twisters that come

To nothing in the squint of the mirror;
Faint as the smile on the watcher's face.

Triptych: Belshazzar's Feast
after Rembrandt's *Belshazzar's Feast c. 1637*

Underneath the city the river flows. Safe as houses
In the swagger of its watchtowers, Babylon
The golden stands as sentinel of the river beds,
Architect of the hanging terraces on an evening

When nothing untoward moves to disturb the horses,
The sleeping dogs. In the shimmering sandstone haze,
Whitened temples sparkle with mosaic tiles the colour
Of camelias; the holy enclosed by ochre bricks

Stacked foursquare against the outside world exactly
As Herodotus had seen, once, from a distance.
Underneath the city, the river carries the secret water
Markings of the subterrain into the arching gardens where,

A stone's throw from the Ishtar Gate, the Israelites
Are keeping their heads down. Listening.

It was the mother of all parties, a never-ending feast
Fuelled by a click of the king's fingers, wine
From the finest vineyards, dishes to die for, the Tower
Of Babel heard in the chattering of the party animals

And the king in fancydress hanging loose in the *savoir-faire*
Of full stomachs to name him master, lord, king of kings.
Belshazzar held nothing back; *click-click-click*
And the golden goblets of Solomon filled to the brim

With Babylonian wine are hoisted to the banqueting hall,
Carried past the threshold where gold patens are kicked
Aside by revellers out of their heads; the god-given golden
Cups snatched by slackened hands, spilled wine

Sticking like resin, like caked blood onto all the fissures
Of the marble. A free for all. One hell of a party.

Suddenly you're the one centre-stage and reeling
From the script written on the plaster of your palace
Wall; suddenly you're the King again, a player
In the dumbshow where the cast of a thousand

Come back to themselves and waken to the blood
Draining from your face, coming to in the dragnet
Of your outstretched arms. A giant in the fading light
Of the wall sconces, they watch you (weak at the knees)

Watching the handwriting lock from left
To right across the opened page of a ghostly ledger,
Watching the ciphers stiffen your mind. Even without
A code, the words still add up as if the fingerbones

Had etched unexpected sanctions on the merry-
Go-round of the party circuit. The price to be paid.

Nemesis

With pen, paper and pockets bulging with words,
Hermes (newly arrived from paradise) sets out his stall
Along familiar faultlines.

Imagine an accident halfway between pen and paper
With debris scattered wide and the silence settling
Back into itself, as it does.
                      And imagine, post-mortem,
The meticulous analysis of fragments that might
Have been a word.
Imagine too the painstaking arrangement of trays
To catch the vapour that remains.

And then he steps out into the dead heat
Of the Old City leading the way to the house
Of the American in the Arab Quarter,
A brown-robed monk used to the twists & turns
(The kind of places to avoid on the climb),
Claiming agency of the unknown, left me
Without a word
                    or a backward glance
Under the lemon tree in the courtyard of a house full
Of the kind of smalltalk that rises like incense and gleans
Sweetness from the lemons, unaware
                    that one day,
Without warning, some unweathered part
Of him would come out of nowhere and surface
Along an Atlantic strand, still on the look-out.

Soul Talk

Above the crackling,
I hear the slow release of soul from an old language
On the radio talkshow;

                    A miracle of loaves
And fishes putting the word out for instant release
On the medium wave,

Going out on air
Without prior recording of voice or tone;
Live, for the first time.

Waking the Dead

1.

If only death were a simple matter
    Of taking the picture cards
        At face value

And going for broke
    In the game of chance
        Beyond the grave,

A hand surrendered and a walk
    Away from the folding table,
        Following suit.

If only the dead could speak,
    Dealing cut nouns
        On the quiet and hiding

Their traces in the bare-faced lie
    Of the cards, the downplay
        Of the discards—

Going through the motions
    Without a show of hands
        Or an opening bid.

And who alive knows
    What will beat the banker
        When the chips are down?

But I imagine the dead as lost for words,
    The mechanics of language
        Of little use in practice

    And the deuce to pay
            In the tournament coming to life
                Before their eyes

    And calling their bluff in a straight flush
        To trounce a full house
            Or five of a kind

In the time it takes to shuffle & cut
        The marked cards, ranked as
              Clichés in cold stone.

2.

What prompted the sleepwalker
    To suddenly break out, bumping
        Into song like that as I passed

Unnoticed? Why nudge that sung miserere
    Past the eye's nightshade
        To where the cry of the banshee

Soars, the score stoking
    Deaf ears, a quaver in the mind
        Of the faithful departed,

When even the faithful know
    White maggots
        In the credo of their days,

And nothing, no sun's orbit or moon,
    No royal flush,
        Or $E=MC$ squared

Trumps anything, proposition or premise
    Notwithstanding; days when Nietzsche alone
        Earns postmortal applause

For his offbeat challenge to the boffins,
    His long-drawn-out waiting
        For cockcrow.

3.

    Was it all in Dante's head
        The schooled imagination
            That produced on cue

A murky river crossing
    Smudged with open boat
        And hooded boatman,

Trading as carriage for all who come
    In turn and out, across
        That pitch-black Acheron?

What then? Fabulous monsters
    And traps to be sidestepped
        On the peril of your life,

The cashing in of chips gained
    Or lost over the lived years
        On the downside,

The spin of demons
    Basking in deranged psyches,
        Or the quest for the ultimate—

That white figure hard to make out
    In its brilliance, archetype
        Of the hour-of-our-death

Drawing each poker-face out
    Beyond the endgame in a blind
        Exit from a round

Staked with regret
    For what might have been,
        Might yet in time be.

4.

    For the life of them, O'Cadhain's dead
        Cannot rest, fretting over
            Lost chances and old scores

In the stony soil beyond Spiddal.
        Granted, nothing much happens
            When you're six feet under

And out of the game; small wonder
        That talk is cheap and rumours about
            Who's in, who's out do the rounds,

Wanting the lowdown on what the living
        Are up to, living over the odds
            With little thought of what's in stock.

Given half a chance, you would have gone
        The same way, would go again throwing
            The same quibbles to the wind

Until spent by some persistent condition
        Or strange malignancy
            Immune to extreme unction.

Comes to us all in the end,
        One way or another,
            Expected or not.

5.

Besides death, there's no other news.
    You knew him, didn't you
        That man who died suddenly

En route to the A & E? Too late.
    Pronounced dead on arrival.
        Nothing to be done

Except inform the next of kin
    Who are sure to ask discreet questions
        About the contents of his pockets

And the possibility of a will. Must
    Have been hearts, even though he held
        The cards close to his chest.

One minute in mid stride, the next
    Deadweight on the ground, listening
        To the siren and wondering

What happened to the time, looking at St. Peter
    And explaining his predicament, trying
        To talk his way out if only

To complete his transactions in the bank,
    Lodge a pocketful of cheques
        Before the end of play.

6.

And suppose St. Peter really did emerge
    To patrol the pearly gates,
        Equipped with a long list

Of questions concerning life on earth
    (Please answer yes or no with a tick
        In the relevant boxes.

And please be patient while our computer
    Downloads your state-of-grace
        And assesses your eternal rest

Since it takes time to tip the balance,
    Adjust your curriculum vitae, especially
        In respect of the final draft).

And suppose his decision was final? (The train
    Waiting at platform three terminates
        In Purgatory. Please have your

Tickets ready for our inspectors). Hell? With no
    Way back, going on and on
        And on…

With paradise running to the clap-happy and
    Suicide bombers en route
        Ad aeternum.

7.

Ask about God dot com
    And every blogger known
        Will post her own notice.

Is this the acceptable face of death,
    Old, grey and bearded, a patriarch
        With the *dies irae*

On his furrowed brow, word made flesh?
    (Anti-feminist to boot—no doubt—goes
        With the territory).

On the other hand, may be a figment
    Of the medieval imagination, a genie
        From the bottle of feverish minds

Caught in the grip of plague
    Or some other punishment
        Ordained by God; not half

Tickled to death at the spin
    Of the roulette wheel and a bid
        On double or quits.

Ring a ring a roses, a pocket
    Full of posies, a tissue, a tissue,
        We all fall down.

8.

Ask any man, there's a very fine line
    Between God and man (no, really)
        With God fingered

On a daily basis whenever something
    Is up for grabs and a pair
        Is needed for the cinch.

Look how the card sharps of history
    Have never missed a trick
        When it comes to hedging

Their bets, eyeballing the takings
    And the wagers placed on two red aces
        And the queen of spades.

May their souls and the souls
    Of all the faithful departed
        Through the mercy of God

Rest in peace. By all accounts, and with oceans
    Of mercy at his disposal, enough to cover
        The universe over and over

God appears, *sotto voce,* as the agent
    Of the possible,
        Dying for a start

And waiting on the throw of the dice
    And the word for go in the game
        Of snakes and ladders.

9.

It's your go. Though not if
        The spun top comes to nought
                Through the play

Of a broken cross. And not before
        I have my say, not
                Before my time.

Reading between the Lines

Somewhere between tide and ebbtide,
The redshank maps out
                     a space
In which to chance a fragile grammar
In a race against time. Who knows which wave

Will drag its debris to the alphabet floor?
And who knows
                     where its secrets
Will beach, and which listener will in time
Astonish with stories halfheard

Through a bivalve or broken seashell, forgotten
Rhythms we once were used to,
                     known to
Reverberate in the telling in the distance between
What I mean, what you think I mean.

Tableau

Regarding that day when you carried
The bureau on your shoulders
From the top floor down

Past the narrowed eyes of the *concierge*
And out into the rainspattered sunlight
Of the *Place*, leaving a trail

Of papers fluttering in the stairwell –
You knew, didn't you

As you watered those plants for the last time
Out on the *terrace* and watched me looking inward
That it was my high altar, my tabernacle?

And by the time the scribbled evidence
Of the paper trail had worn thin and vanished
Into raindrops and the scramble for missing words
Had panned out across acres of black sea,

Your memory had settled into the amber of mine.
And that day, when you carried a dream
On your shoulders, became *je ne sais quoi*:

A moment rivetted in the *Seizième*, resting
On the premise in your eyes,
Your murmured words *"de rien, de rien"*.

La Lutte avec l'Ange
after Delacroix, *"La Lutte de Jacob avec l'ange"*, 1861

Wrestling with a messenger in the early hours was not
Jacob's idea of a good night's sleep
And he would have cried off, pleading old age,
Tiredness, time of night
But the Angel insisted, having the wind at his back
And knowing full well
He was more than a match for an old man
Nearing the end of his journey
And hoping at most for the balm of hyssop or myrrh,
The clasp of an arm,
                        but still full of himself
So that he rallied, rounded on the creature
And set to, getting to grips first
With the shadow-play, then locking hard against solid
Blocks of oxygen and the shoulder
Of a spectre blowing hot breath into his face. By night's
End, the night's question
Had came through into the open and hovered in the air
Between them: the one nameless, the other
Lamed, giving way to his new, his given name.

The Home Stretch

One hundred tealights
At a knock-down price:

Picture them glimmering
At the end of a grim December

Picking up
Where the light leaves off.

Image them waltzing
On a slabbed window-sill

Between the end-of-season sky
And the blotched line

Of that easily lost-sight-of horizon

About to capitulate under the weight
Of an *après*-solstice;

And knowing that moment of panic
As Odysseus did catching

Sight of so many yellow ribbons
While gauging the short stretch that came

Between him and what might have been
Ithaca in the mist, bowed to

The necessary going under
Before the sprint, the final run.

Death of Socrates

Even though he made a name for himself
With the corner boys, always asking
The same question and in such a roundabout way
That they couldn't make head nor tail
Of what he was getting at, he hadn't the sense
Of a child when it came to the real world, nor
The sense to know that there are people who like
Questions.
                      And people who don't.
And even when they handed him the cup
With enough poison in it to wipe out all the rats
In Athens, he spent all the time he had left talking,
Talking, drawing them out into the heartbeat
Of the question and demanding to know
Whether they thought it was better to die
In the right than in the wrong. Like they cared.

Double Take

Echo never wanted the last word but it was all
She was left with; opening her mouth to speak
Was not part of the deal. So, she stopped short

Of sounding out the words and suffered the loss.
And she dreamed. Of a full purse and a spending spree
From the far side of silence, an escape from the last

Pair of see-saw fricatives which always got in the way
Of the hoped-for *open sesame*: the green light signalling
Go and the sudden onrush as word and meaning

Dived into the same ocean and swam for it. Dipping
Her toe in the pool, who did she meet but Narcissus
In the grip of his doppelganger? Lost for words.

❧

They named him Narcissus believing him to be
A navel-gazer of sorts, when all he was trying to do
Was fix the image as any photographer would.

As he would have done somehow if he hadn't slipped,
Shattering the lens as he fell headlong into the *camera
Obscura* of the mountain pool. Out like a light.

A moment frozen in time and placed on record
As a salutary reminder to those who tinker
With images. And miss the point.

Who can capture the static in a one-dimensional print,
The divine transmission in shadow? We wait for the sun
And moon to coalesce. Meanwhile, first things first.

Heidegger's Silence

> "Whereof one cannot speak, thereof one must be silent"
> —Wittgenstein

What kind of coming so distracted the man
In the thinker's cap that he did—not—
See the galloping horsemen acquire

The house of numbers, the cobbler's
Brazen eyes once again dreaming nails
Into flesh, or old tomes going up in smoke?

*Take a fistful of words and scatter them
Like dice across a chequerboard knowing the dice
Are loaded and will land exactly as planned.
Call it language management or the like—jargon,
Asides from the inside track, office talk.*

*Consider such a process from the point
Of view of logistics, as if the numbers referred to
Were crates transported to a railway
Siding as an interim measure, a hitch in the handling
Of goods in transit.*

What kind of testament so distracted the man
In the thinker's cap that he
Did not see, not then or later when, on home ground

The poet's[1] smothered words
Floated like quenched candles on the waters
Of the *Rive Gauche,* oceanbound?

---

[1] Paul Celan

Wrong Address

When I called, you were out
Counting as many stars
As you could find
On a dark night.

When I left, you were still out
With your back to the fire
Counting on loose change
And a day's walk.